# Edward Elgar
## SERENADE FOR STRINGS
### Op. 20
Edited by
Richard W. Sargeant, Jr.

Study Score
Partitur

SERENISSIMA MUSIC, INC.

# ORCHESTRA

Violin I

Violin II

Viola

Violoncello

Double Bass

Duration: ca. 12 minutes
Premiere: March 1892
Worcester, United Kingdom
Worcester Ladies' Orchestral Class / Composer

ISMN: 979-0-58042-111-1
Composed between 1888 and 1892. This score is anewly-engraved edition based upon the first edition
full score and parts issued in 1893 by Breitkopf und Härtel, Leipzig.

# SERENADE
## for String Orchestra
### Op. 20

**1.**

Edward Elgar
Edited by Richard W. Sargeant, Jr.

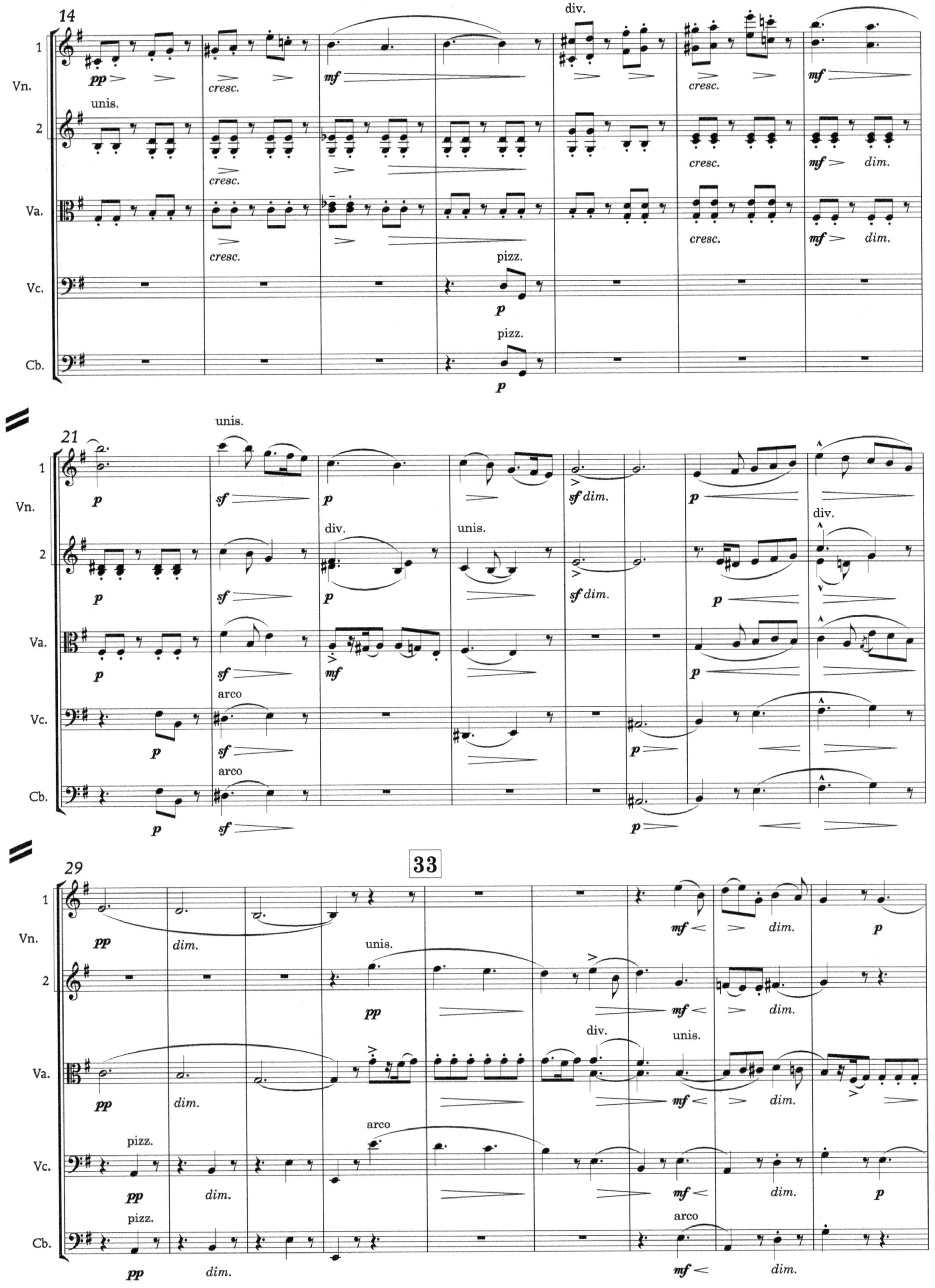
14
Vn. 1 2
Va.
Vc.
Cb.
unis.
div.
pizz.
pp
cresc.
mf
dim.
p
21
unis.
div.
arco
sf
sf dim.
29
33
pp
dim.
mf

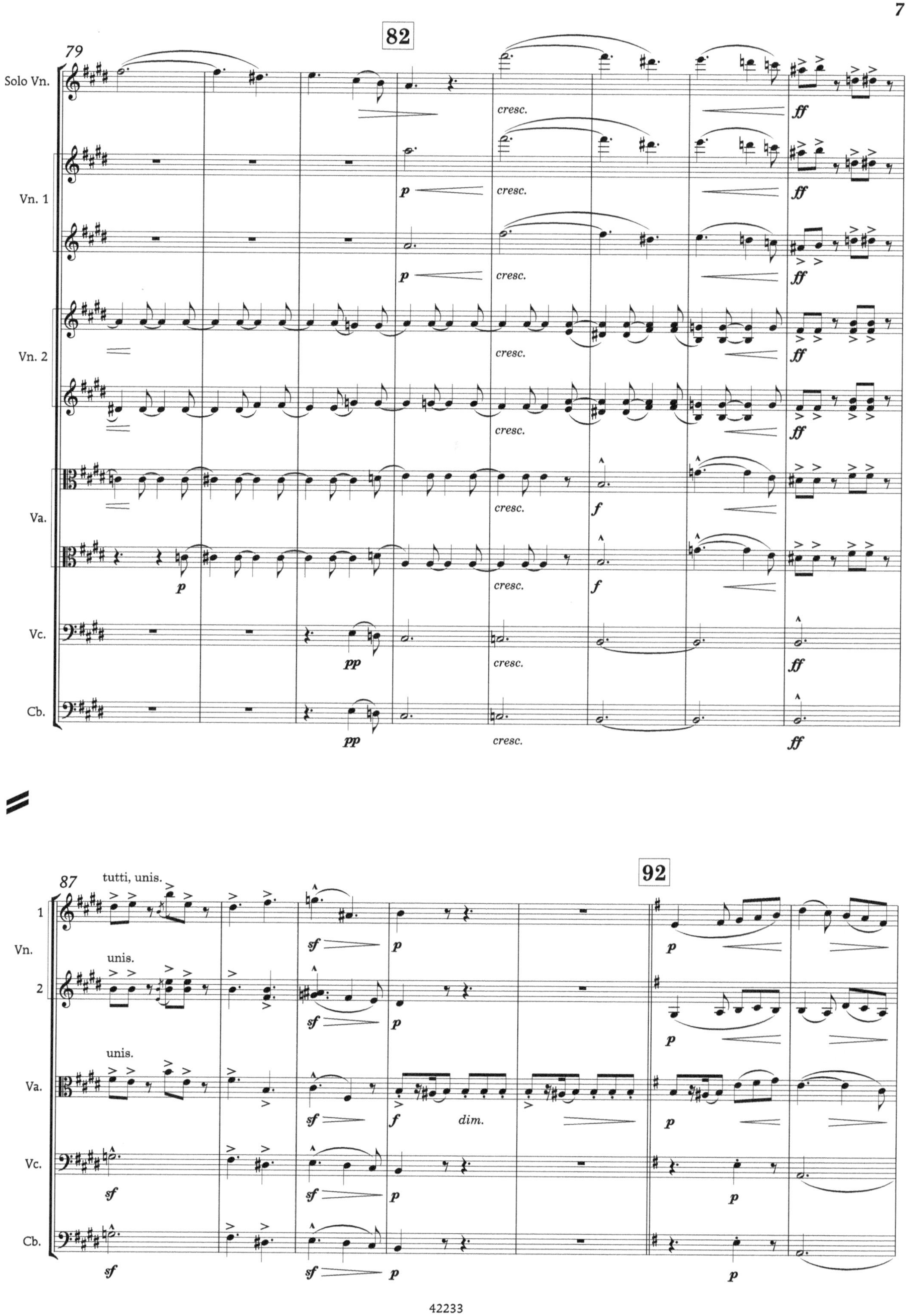

79
82
Solo Vn.
Vn. 1
Vn. 2
Va.
Vc.
Cb.
cresc.
p
f
ff
pp
87
92
tutti, unis.
unis.
Vn.
1
2
sf
dim.

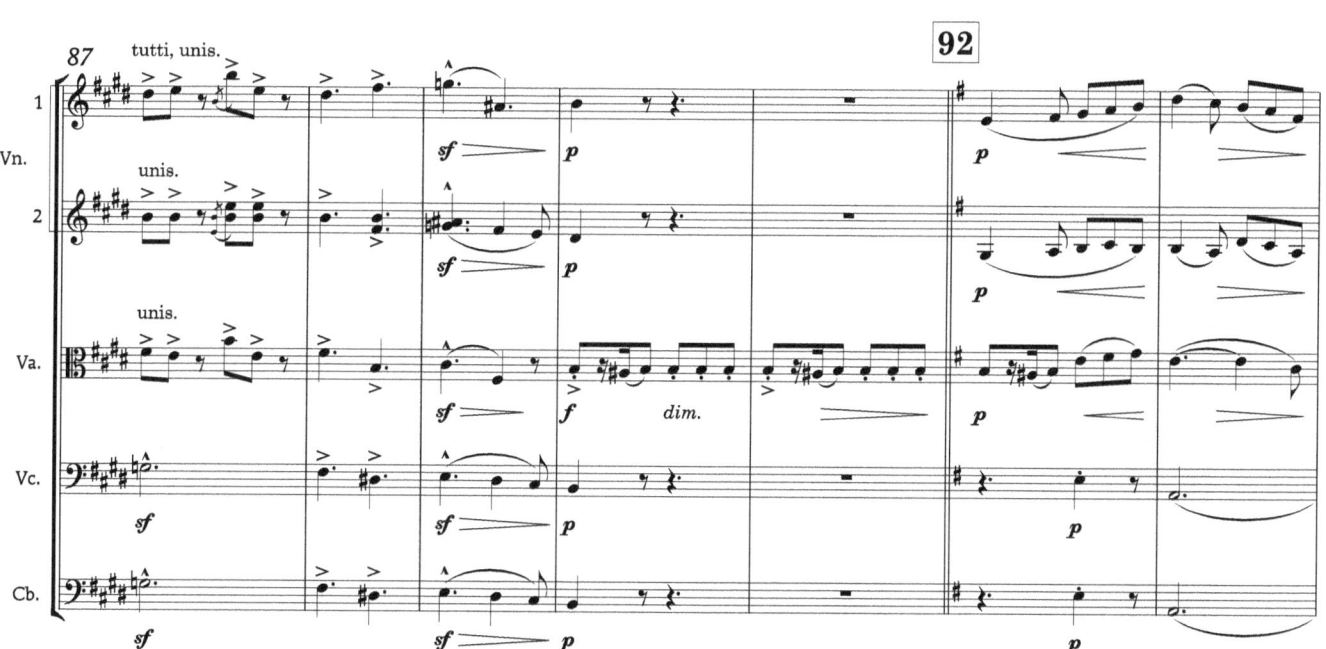

8

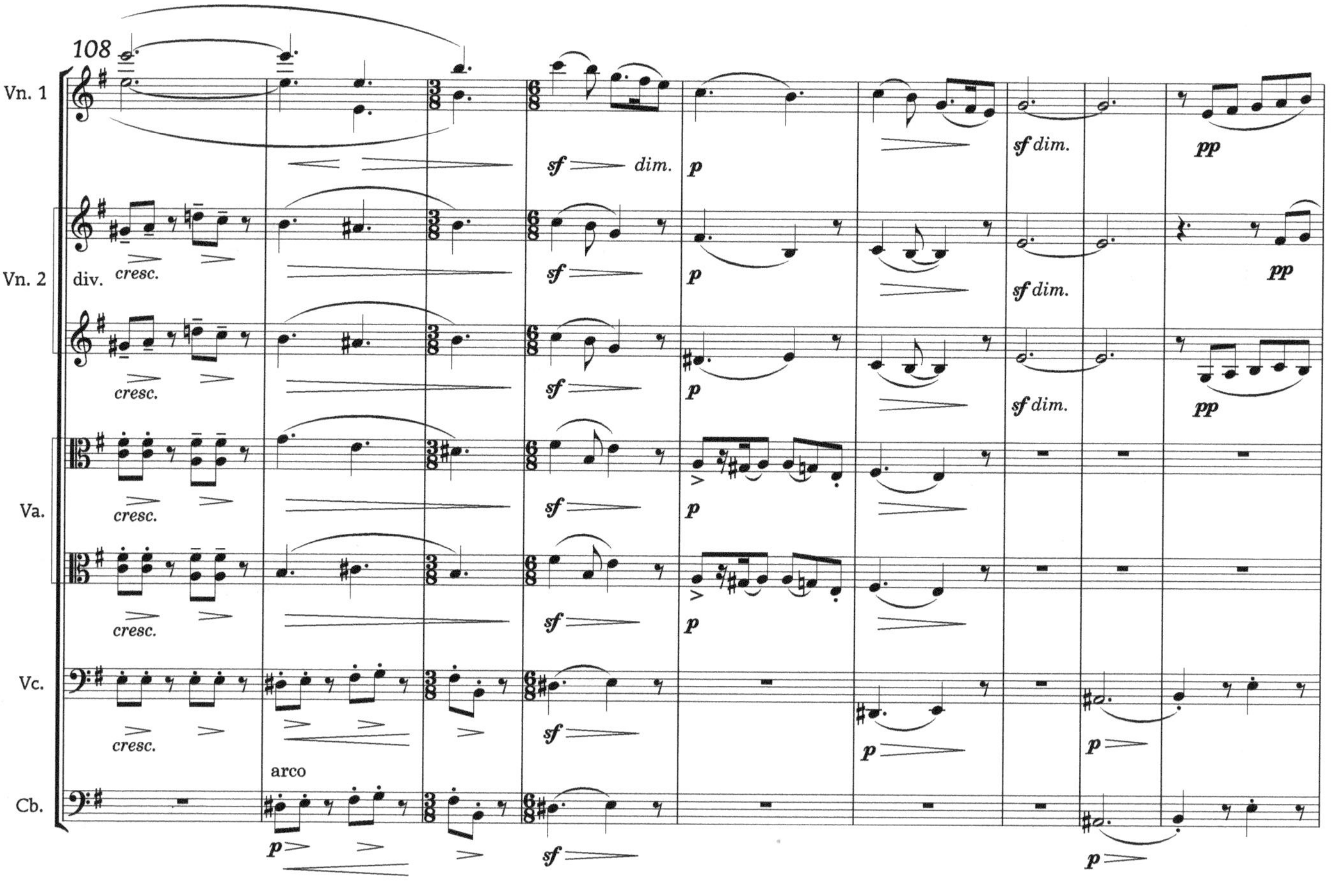
108
Vn. 1
Vn. 2
div.
cresc.
Va.
Vc.
Cb.
arco
dim.
sf dim.


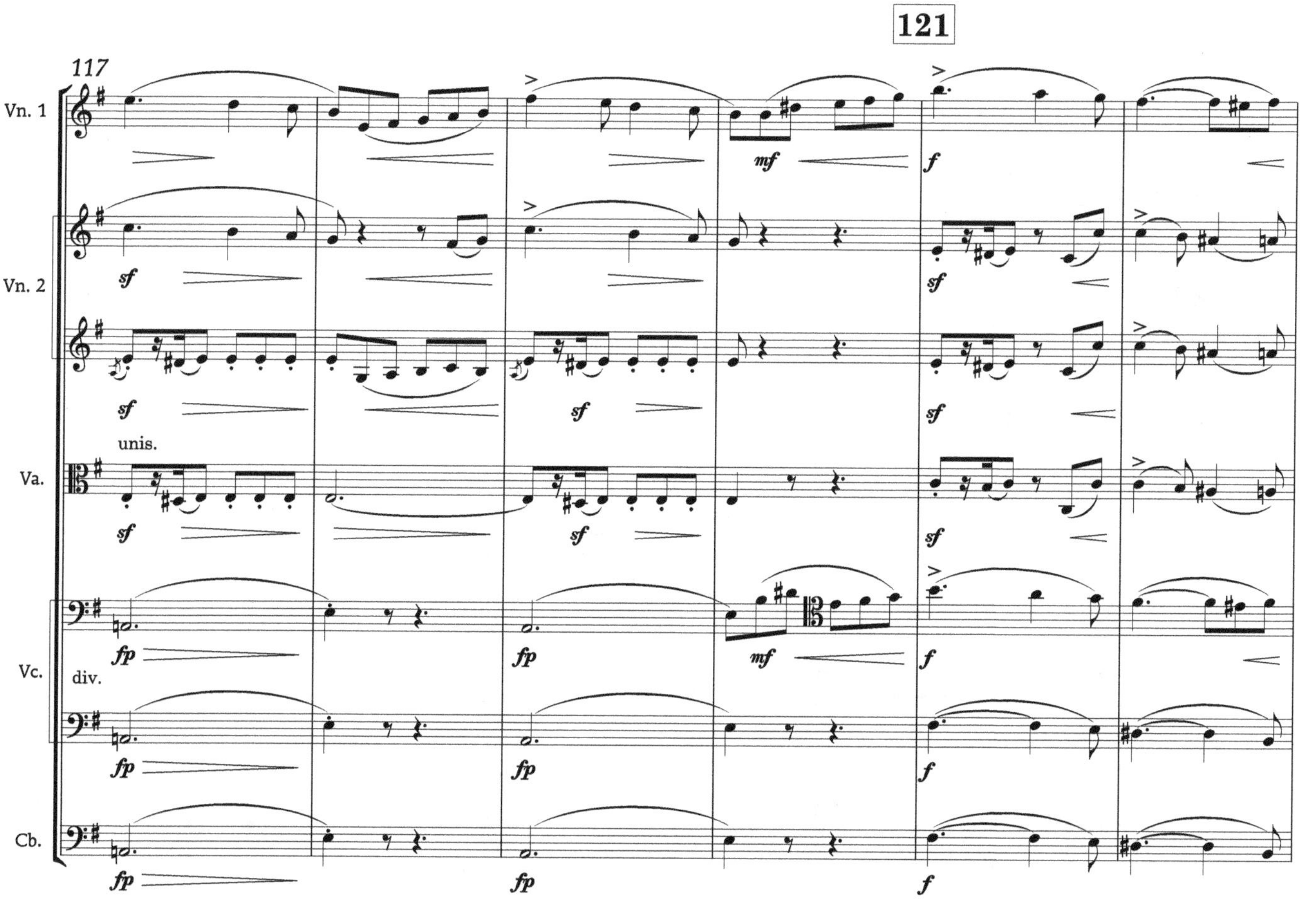
121
117
Vn. 1
Vn. 2
Va.
unis.
Vc.
div.
Cb.

## 2.

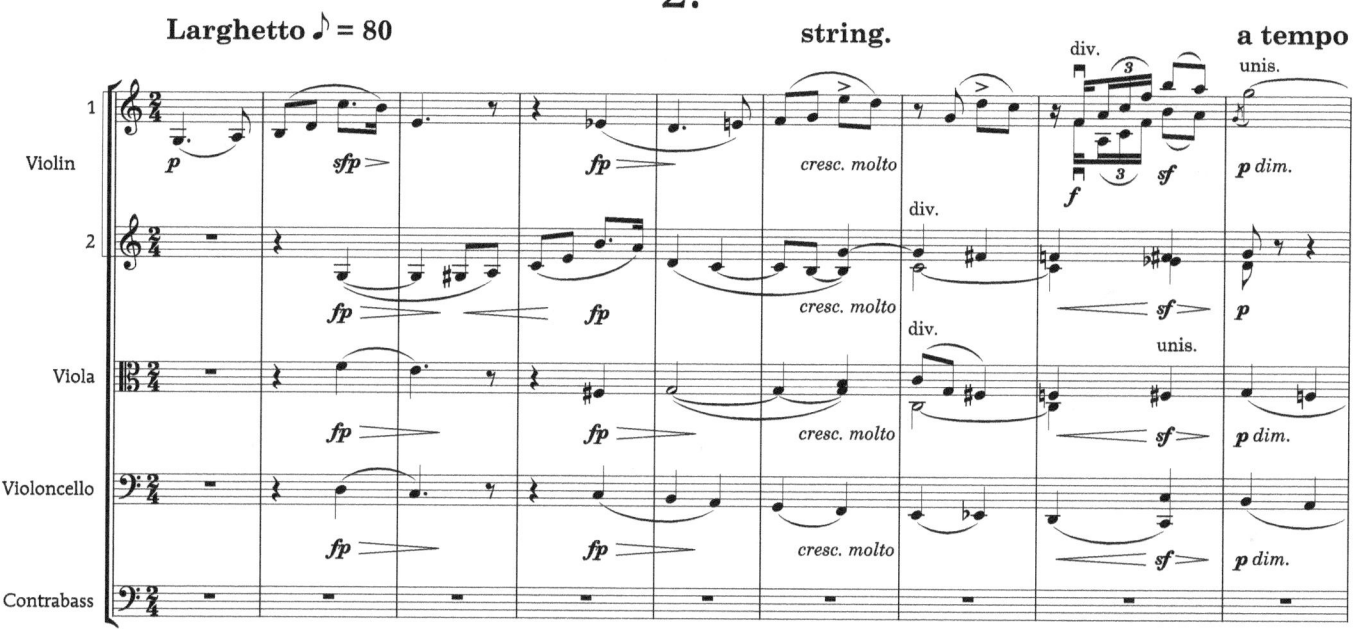
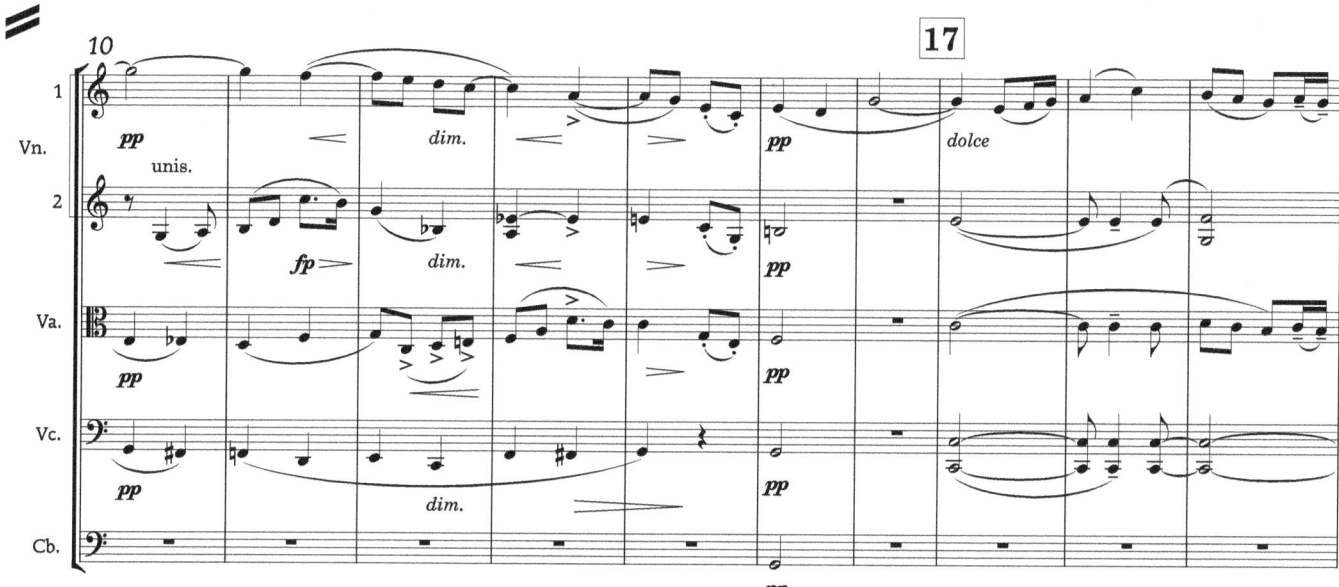

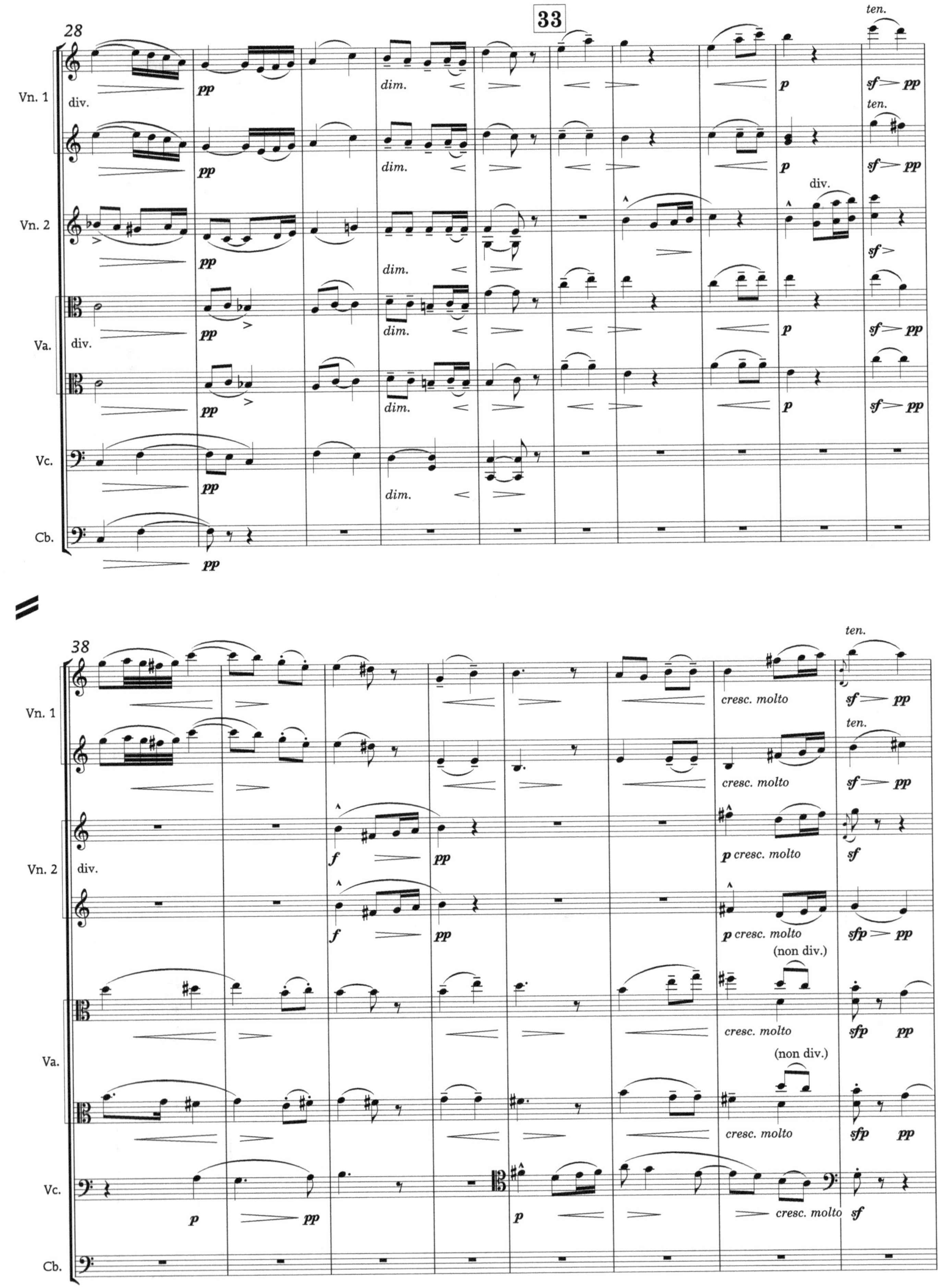
28
33
ten.
Vn. 1
div.
pp
dim.
sf
p
Vn. 2
Va.
Vc.
Cb.
38
cresc. molto
p cresc. molto
sfp
(non div.)
f

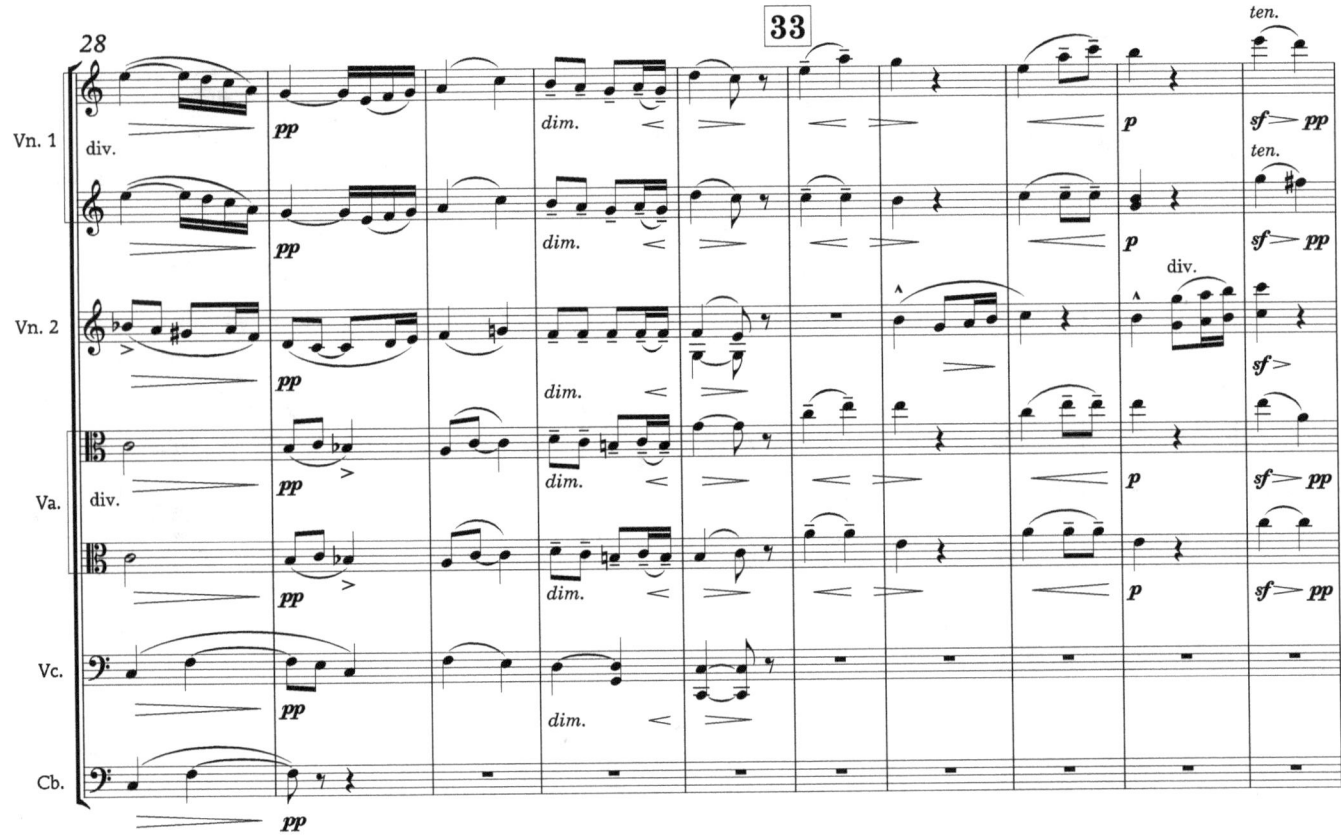

poco rit.
51
a tempo
46
Vn. 1
Vn. 2
Va.
Vc.
Cb.
unis.
ppp
pp
pp > ppp
52
div.
cresc.
ppp cresc.

56
ten.
Vn. 1
rf
f
Vn. 2
Va.
Vc.
Cb.
unis.
60
1
Vn.
2
p
Va.
Vc.
Cb.

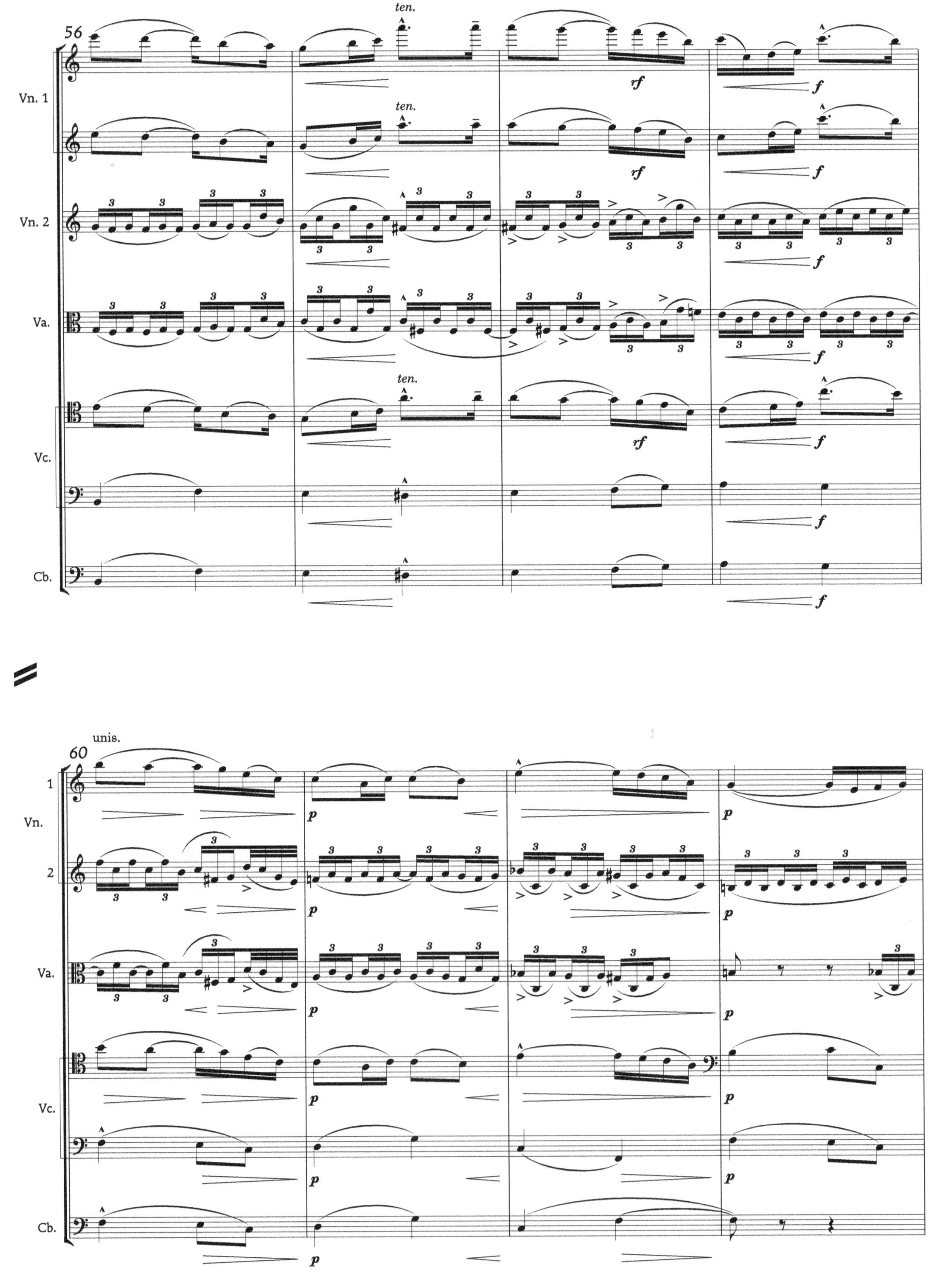

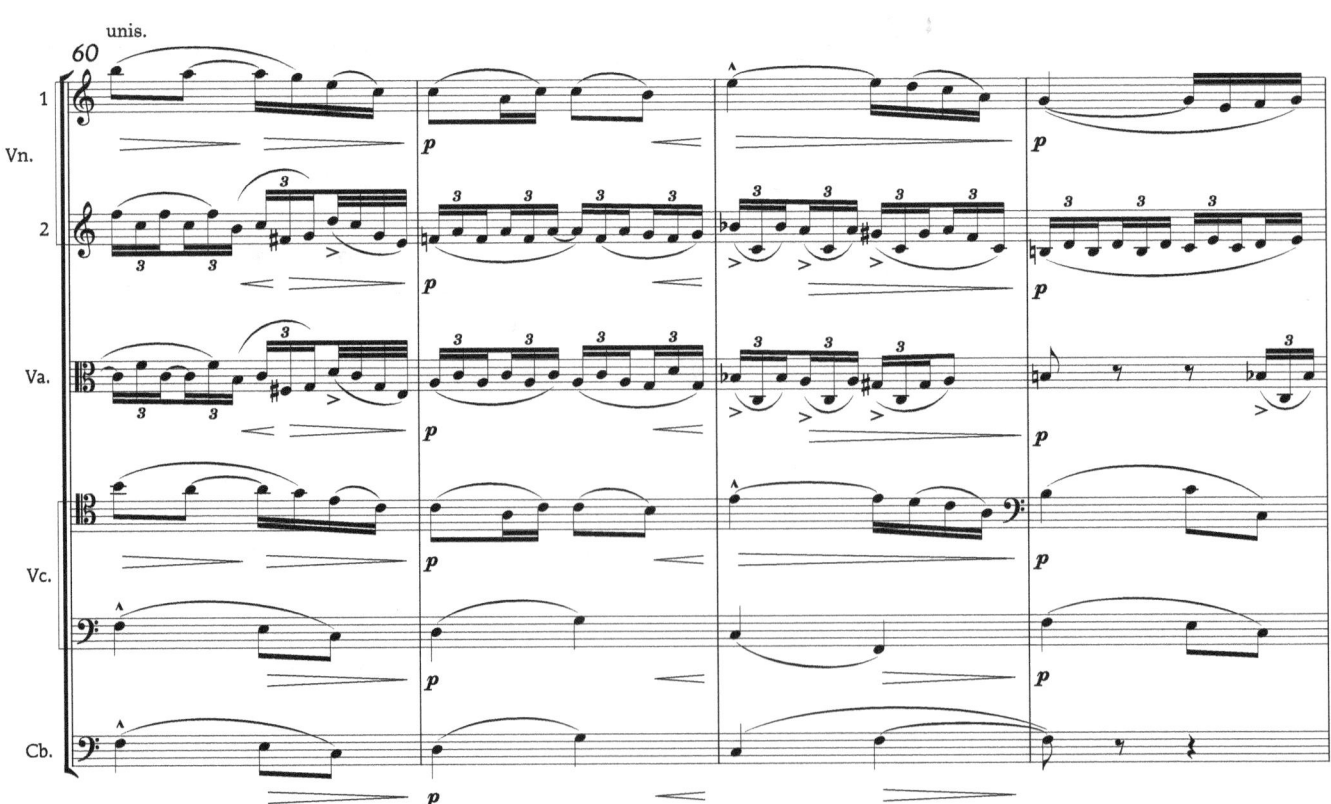

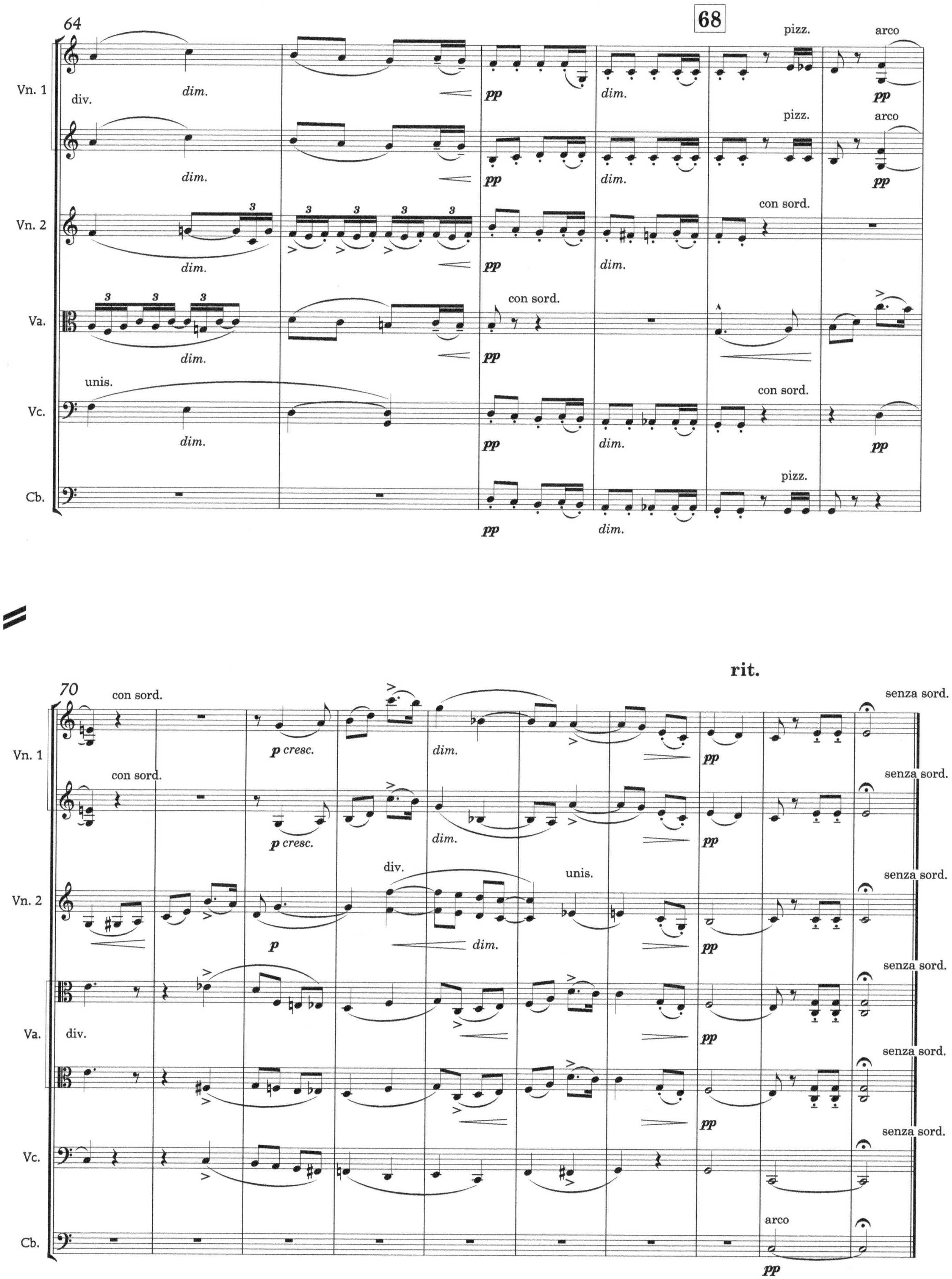
64
68
Vn. 1
Vn. 2
Va.
Vc.
Cb.
div.
dim.
pp
pizz.
arco
con sord.
unis.
70
rit.
p cresc.
p
senza sord.

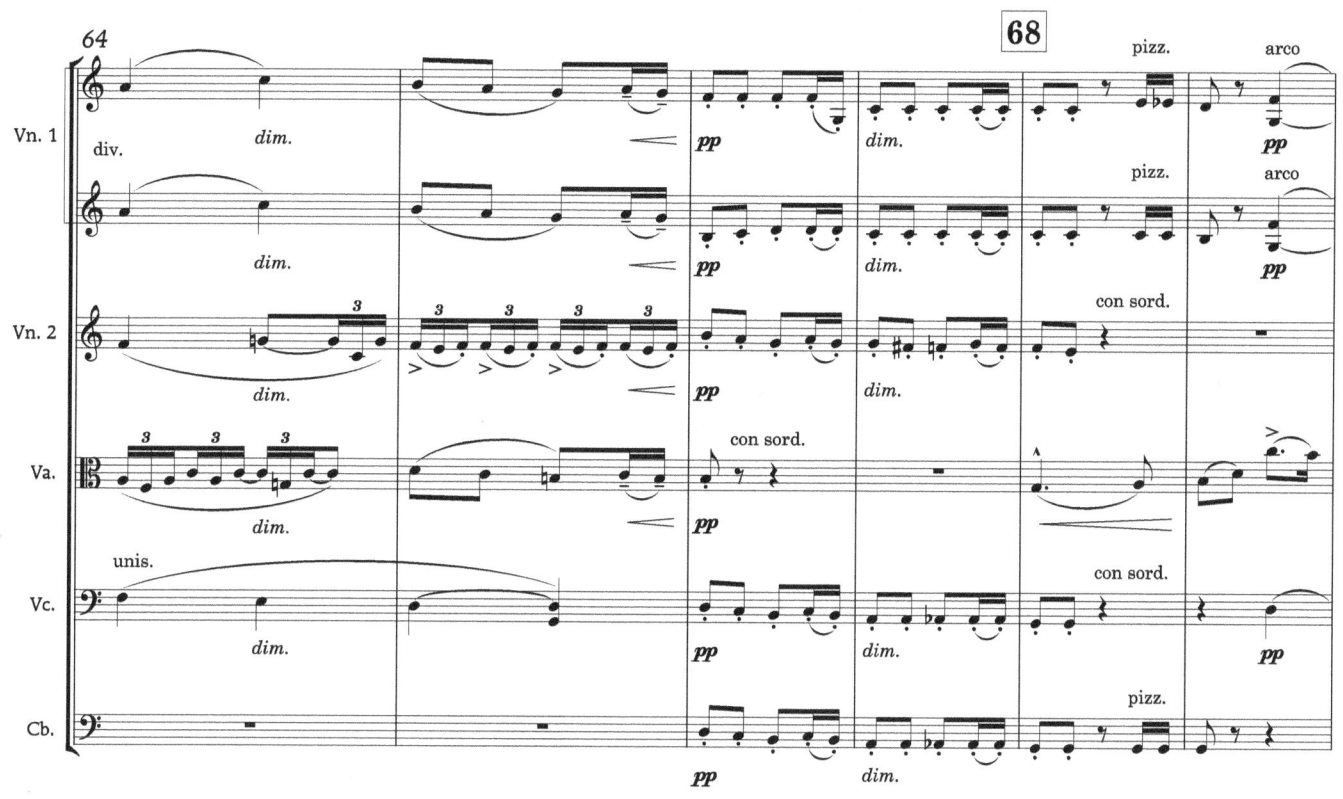

# 3.

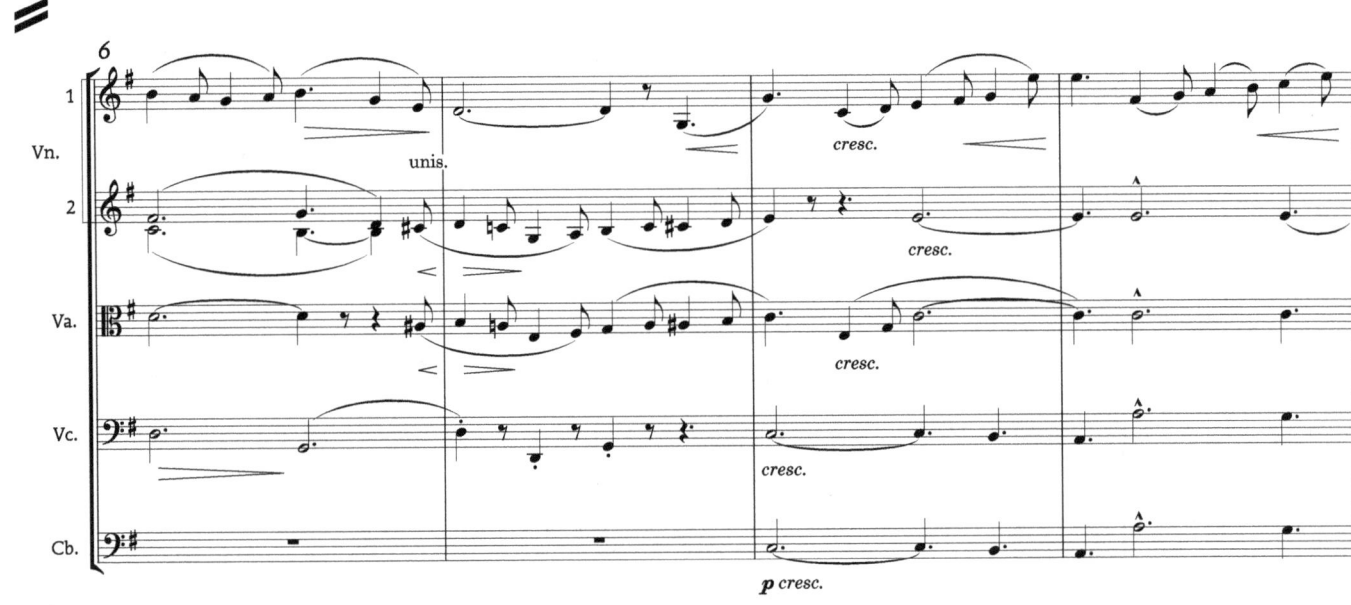

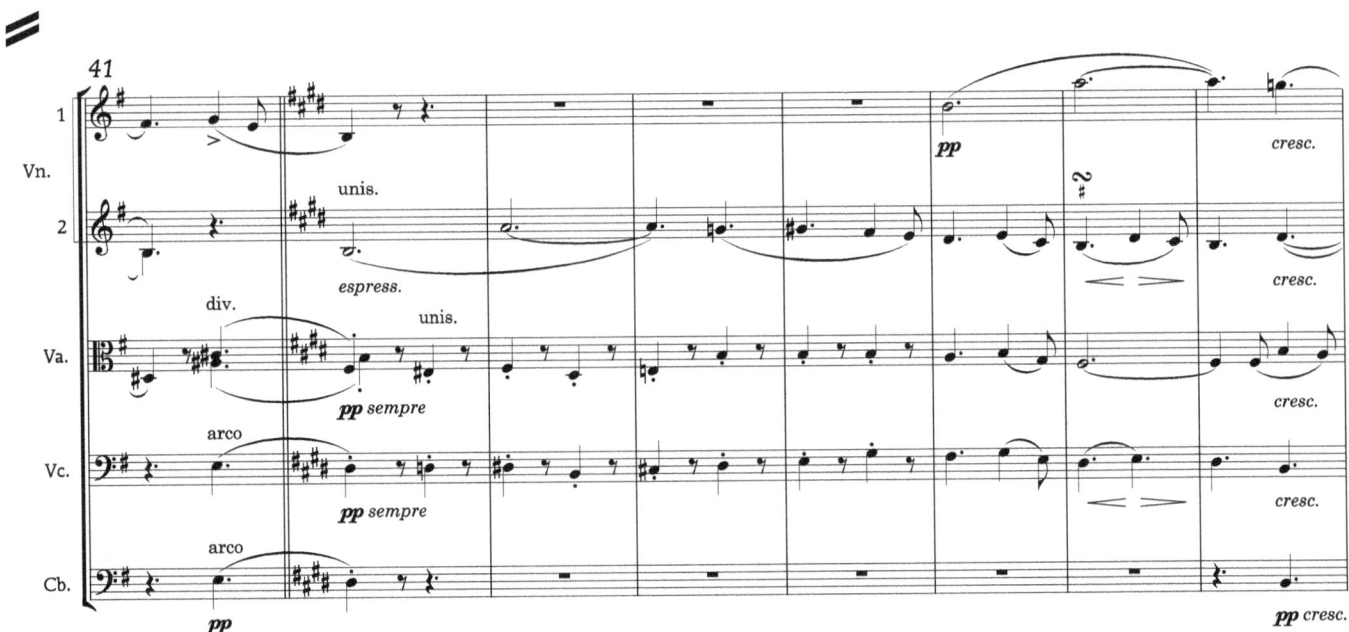

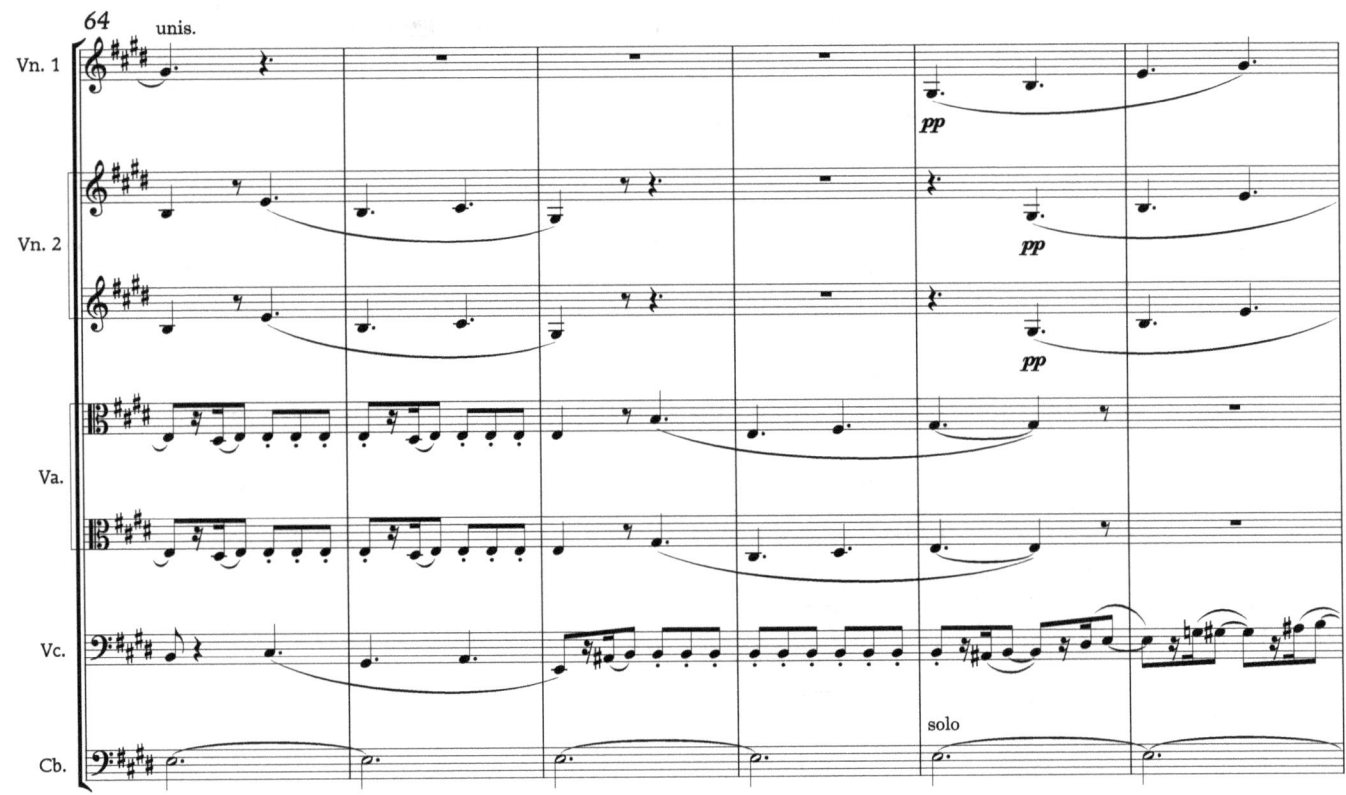

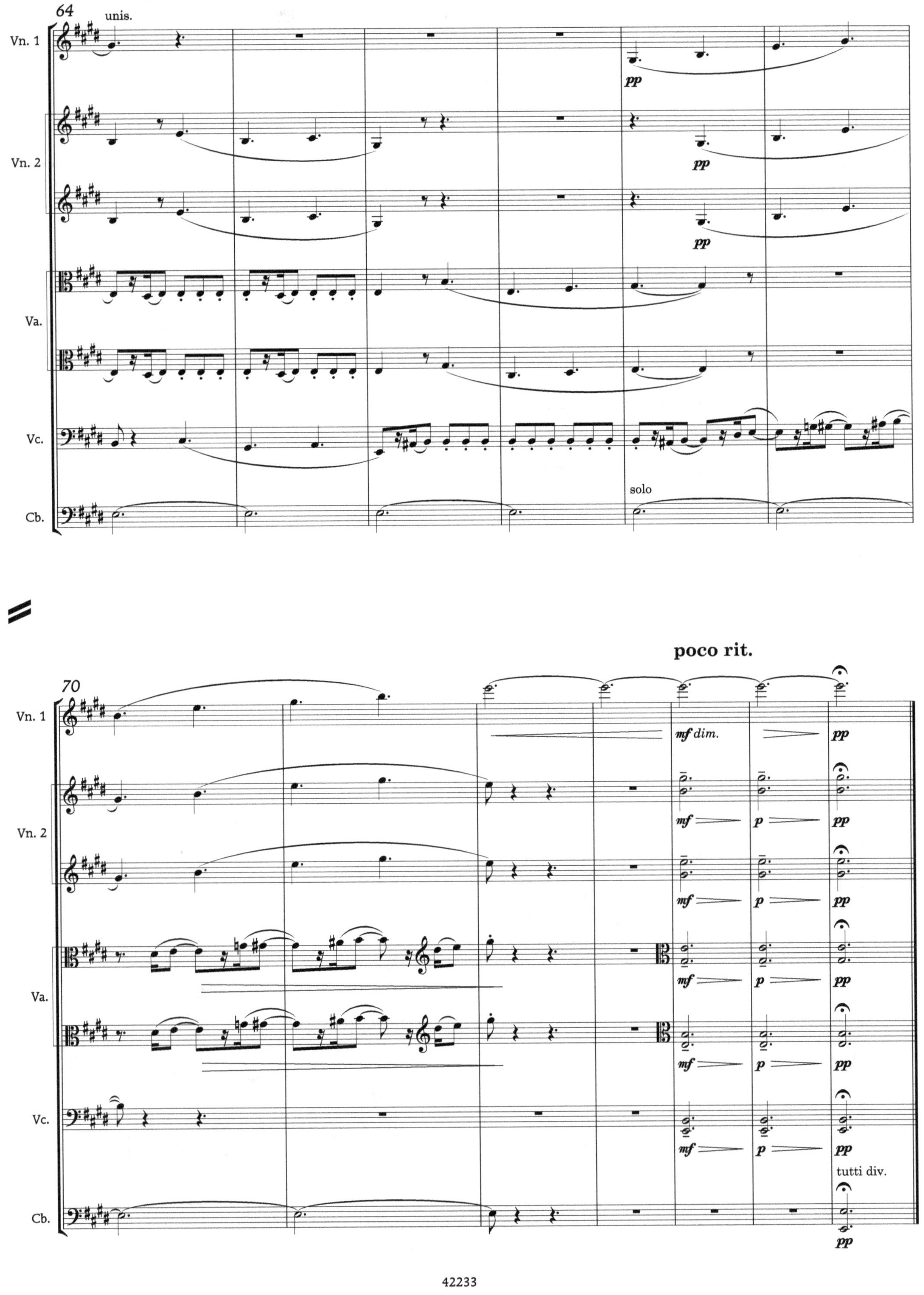
64
unis.
Vn. 1
Vn. 2
Va.
Vc.
Cb.
pp
pp
pp
solo
poco rit.
70
mf dim.
mf
p
pp
tutti div.

www.ingramcontent.com/pod-product-compliance
Lightning Source LLC
Chambersburg PA
CBHW081026040426
42444CB00014B/3373